How to Survive Your Grief

When Someone You Love Has Died

Susan L. Fuller

How to Survive Your Grief
When Someone You Love Has Died

For permissions, contact
Susan L. Fuller
P.O. Box 35
Wood River Junction, RI 02894
susan@susanfuller.com

Printed in the United States

ISBN: 9781441450227

Library of Congress Registration: TX 6-860-376

First Printing 2008

This book is dedicated to all of my clients
who have taught me
what this journey of grief and healing is all about.

To join a 'Survive Your Grief Support Group', please contact me at

susan@susanfuller.com

To order addtional copies. please visit me at:

http://www.SurviveYourGrief.com

.

HOW TO USE THIS BOOK

The information in this book is not meant to make the pain go away. It is meant to help you understand what you're feeling, why it's useful, and how to move through it as quickly and healthfully as possible.

This book was not written to be read from beginning to end. Rather it's designed so you can dip in and find exactly what you need when you need it. I hope you will find it helpful when you are feeling confused, uncertain, and in need of reassurance.

When you're grieving, it can be hard to focus, so the book is divided into short sections with important points highlighted.

Responses to grief are so particular to the individual involved, that some of this material may not apply to you. Please take what is useful to you and leave the rest.

A Note About Violent and Unexpected Deaths

This book was written to help those going through a normal grieving process. By its nature, violent and unexpected death such as suicide or homicide, bring with it, complications that go beyond normal grieving. Although you may find many parts of this book helpful, it is probably not enough to fully support you in the special issues related to these kinds of deaths.

TABLE OF CONTENTS

"The emotional pain caused by loss suffered does not move toward forgetfulness. It moves, rather, in the direction of enriched remembrance; the memory becomes an integral part of the mourner's personality. The work of mourning has been completed when the person (or cherished thing) no longer appears as an absence in a barren world, but has come to reside securely within one's heart. Each of us must grieve in his own manner and at his own pace. For many people, one year seems to bring completion. Others require much more or much less time. Periodic waves of grief are often felt for the remainder of ones life. The mourning process must be given the freedom to find its own depth and rhythm; it cannot be artificially accelerated. A loss, like a physical wound, cannot heal overnight. There is *no way to hurry the stages of tissue growth, and there is no way to speed up the healing process of mourning. But, when mourning has been completed, the mourner comes to feel the inner presence of the loved one, no longer an idealized hero or a maligned villain, but a presence with human dimensions. Lost irreversibly in objective time, the person is present in a new form within one's mind and heart, tenderly present in inner time without the pain and bitterness of death. Once the loved one has been accepted in this way, he can never again be forcefully removed."*

Robert Chernin Cantor, <u>And a Time to Live: Toward Emotional Well-Being during the Crisis of Cancer</u>, Harper & Row, 1978.

INTRODUCTION

In my work with the grieving, the number one question I hear is, "I feel like I'm going crazy. Is this normal?"

For the vast majority of people, the answer is, "Yes, it's normal."

Normal grief can certainly feel a lot like 'going crazy', but when you think about the magnitude of your loss, would any other response be appropriate? Doesn't it seem crazier to go on with your life as if nothing had happened, as if the ground underneath you hadn't disappeared in a single breathe?

The truth is, that by some miracle which speaks to the strength and fortitude of the human heart, we do survive and even thrive following the death of someone we love. Every day, you make it through somehow, even when it feels like you're slogging through quicksand, but over time, you regain your equilibrium and slowly begin to reinvest in life.

I know it's hard to believe right now while you're in the midst of it, and it may not be particularly helpful, but it is the truth nonetheless.

Grief is a Most Trustworthy Companion

Personally, I have lost both parents, grandparents, beloved pets and a marriage. I know about loss because I've experienced it.

As a bereavement counselor and support group facilitator, I have had the profound privilege of sharing this journey with hundreds of people who were grieving just like you. Being a witness for those suffering a recent loss has left me with nothing less than awe at the wisdom of the grieving process.

Grief knows the way.

Your job is to follow where it leads. Grief knows exactly what you need and when. It will guide you every step of the way if you're willing to follow. Allowing yourself to experience the tumultuous tidal wave of feelings is the fastest and surest way out of the pain.

It sounds counterintuitive, doesn't it?

Think of it this way. When you experience physical pain, tensing the muscles around the pain increases the experience of pain and does nothing to hasten the healing of a physical wound. The same is true of emotional pain. When we try to shut ourselves off from the pain, it increases the agony and prolongs the healing.

That's not to say there won't be times you want to shut down and times that you will. Sometimes, it's just too much. That's part of the process too.

Healing grief is a lot like healing a physical wound. We don't question that a cut finger or a broken bone will heal.

We know that the body will heal itself without much intervention. In most cases, grief will heal itself in time as well.

Sometimes as with serious physical injuries, the intervention of well trained experts is necessary, but even in these cases, much relies on the body's capacity to heal itself. Complicated grief is no different. You may need support to get through it, but ultimately, it is your grief that will heal you.

And yes, grief leaves scars just like some physical injuries, but they are rarely of the big and ugly variety.

Your loss is profound. The pain is profound. It takes courage to grieve. Sometimes it takes blind faith to believe that there is any wisdom strong enough to lead us back into life. But there you have it. In the end, your grief will heal you.

What's Normal?

The most common description I've heard is that grief is like a roller coaster. Others describe it as a tidal wave, but no matter how you describe it, it is a tumultuous process with many varied and contradictory facets. One minute you're in tears, the next you're in a rage, then you're laughing at some memory, and the next thing you know, you're in tears again. Sometimes, you even forget only to be hit again with a new wave grief that brings you to your knees.

The first step in surviving is to acknowledge all of this as absolutely normal. You are undoubtedly experiencing many of the responses listed below and it's important to recognize them for what they are--normal and natural signs of grief, not your ticket to the funny farm.

Grief is a normal and natural response to a traumatic loss. Period! It is not a disease. It is not a psychological disorder. It is a healthy response to the death of someone dear to you.

If in doubt, the one true test of whether your experience is normal is this; if it's moving, it's normal. Normal grief has a fluidity about it that is clearly discernible, especially to those observing it. If you are all over the map, there's generally nothing to worry about.

It's more a feeling of movement than a list you can check off as tasks are accomplished. The movement I'm talking about is not at all linear. Even if you feel like you're going around in circles with little forward motion, it is normal as long as it's moving. Normal grief is fluid, changeable and inconsistent.

The only people who give me any cause for concern are those whose grief never seems to change. Month after month, the emotional expression remains the same without any variance. You may have seen it. It's like someone taking on the static posture of grief rather than moving though it as the dynamic and varied process it is.

It's certainly possible to feel like it isn't changing when in fact it is. Supportive friends, the kind who listen, not the ones offering platitudes so you'll just get over it, can be immensely helpful by mirroring back your progress when you can't see it yet.

Unless your grief feels like it's set in concrete, there's probably no cause for concern. No matter how crazy it might seem, as long as it's moving, it's normal.

How Long Does It Take?

How long it takes depends on many factors, and is as unique to you as your relationship was to the person who has died. For some, a year is sufficient, but for many, it takes considerably longer. There may be times, years later, when you experience a renewed sense of loss. This is normal and generally happens in an instant and is gone as fast as it came. Rarely will it be with the same raw intensity of early grief, but will be experienced more as a nostalgia for who and what was lost.

Interestingly, the more grief is researched, the longer what is considered normal becomes. That's why putting unrealistic time expectations on this process is totally counterproductive. So much depends on you, your relationship with the person who died, the support systems you have in place, and your ability to be open to the pain. There are so many variables that can impact the process of grieving, it is virtually impossible to predict how long your grief will last.

How Will I Know When I'm Done?

Truthfully, it's never completely done because we always remember. The person you love lives on in your heart, but there will always be moments of missing them.

Healing through grief does not mean remaining unchanged. Death changes us and has life altering consequences for everyone touched by it. Life never goes back to the way it was. Much of the grieving process is about discovering a new normal.

Grief is the process of making meaning, if not sense, out of what has happened, and figuring out, heart and mind together, how to move on without the person we so dearly love.

So how do you know you're done? You'll know you're done when you find yourself reinvesting in life. Relationships and activities that have felt void of meaning begin to feel meaningful again. You will find yourself, rather unexpectedly at times, looking forward to the future, and you will find yourself looking back with love.

WHAT CAN I EXPECT:
MODELS AND TASKS OF GRIEF

Everyone grieves differently and at their own pace. There is no right way or wrong way, just your way.

The only viable criteria for assessing whether you're moving through your grief is not some artificial time frame, but whether the process feels fluid. If your grief keeps moving and changing, even if it cycles back, you can be assured you're on the right track.

Containing this normal flow of thought, emotion and experience are very loosely defined stages. These are not set in stone, and your experience may vary quite a bit. Variations do not mean you're off track. It just means your timing is different. Remember if it feels like it's moving and feels unpredictable, you are on track no matter what the time frame.

Whether each stage takes a few weeks, a few months, or even years, grief generally follows this course:

1. Shock and Denial

Just like the body goes into shock following a physical injury, so the mind and emotions go into shock after a death. This is a good thing. Yes, a very good thing. Death is so big that if we took it in all at once, we really would go crazy. So our psyche protects us by blocking out the full reality and giving it to us in bite size bits.

At first, the death can seem so unreal, something like being in a dream. We go through all the motions of our funeral rituals while feeling a bit like Alice in the looking glass. Reactions like thinking you see them, talking to them, feeling their presence, picking up the phone to call them, all tend to happen soon after the death.

The task at this stage is for the loss to become real. This is why funeral rituals are so important. It's why seeing the body can be so important. It's the beginning of making the loss real.

Feeling numb, not being able to cry, feeling lethargic, and forgetting the death has happened are all typical experiences of this time.

It generally takes several months (typically 3-6 months) to move through this phase. You don't need to do anything to move this along. This is a process that unfolds quite naturally. You will move through the fog when you're ready to do so, and not a moment sooner. Trust that you have the inner wisdom to know what you need and to follow it.

2. Active Grieving

Active grieving is sometimes described as disorganization. This is when all of the feelings surface with excruciating intensity. The shock has worn off and you know the person you love is gone. You really know it with every fiber of your being.

The worst part is that the reality hits just as the friends and other supports start to drift away. Insensitive people have been known to say things like "Don't you think it's time you got over it?" when it's really just beginning.

During this phase, the task is to make sense out of the death and the chaotic upheaval it has caused in your life.

Characteristic of this time is the vast array of conflicting and confusing emotions. Just when you seem to be feeling better, you are bombarded with intense emotions, anger, guilt, fear, and just plain pain. It can feel like it's never going to get better. It will get better, but hearing that doesn't help.

This is the time you may really begin to wonder about your sanity. There is often an internal sense that you should be getting over it. This is reinforced by pressure from well meaning friends to move on, to clear out, or to make decisions. Do not succumb to the pressure. That's not at all what you need right now. Right now, you need to be present to all of those squirmy feelings.

The task at this stage is to come to terms with your loss. It's a time of finishing unfinished business with the person who died. It's a messy time of integrating the loss and your feelings about it into the flickering awareness of the new normal that's just beginning to emerge.

Much of the time, this grief feels completely and utterly impossible to deal with in any sane way, never mind actually surviving it and thriving in the future. If you try to manage it, control it, direct it, or pretend it isn't happening, it is impossible. This is a time of surrendering to it all and letting your grief take you where you need to go. It can feel a bit like white water rafting, but in the end, the turmoil starts taking a recognizable shape and form which points to a new life without the person you love.

It is virtually impossible to see how exquisitely wise grief is until you look back on this time. This is the work of the heart and it's happening every minute of every day, whether you're conscious of it or not. Unless you remain shut down to the emotions, your grief will lead you to exactly where you need to go.

Most people don't notice when this phase is coming to an end, but at some point, you'll start thinking about the future. At first, it may be just a stray thought here and there, then a smattering of ideas which finally emerge as real plans for the future.

This has nothing to do with forcing yourself to get over it. It's about allowing a natural transition to take place in which you genuinely begin to think about the things you'd like to do when this is over. This is a normal and natural transition that happens when you stay with the process. Without even knowing it, you start talking in the future tense.

3. Resolution

Resolution is sometimes referred to as reorganization. It is when you begin to feel like yourself again, admittedly a new self, but yourself nonetheless. Life begins to feel normal again. The death becomes woven into the fabric of your life, not as something alien, but as a part of you and your life experience. Your memories of the person who died support your life rather than being painful reminders of what you lost. The complete and utter turmoil of your grief recedes.

For many, but not all, this easing of the grief coincides with the first anniversary of the death. Anticipating that first anniversary often plunges people back into the grief. It can be quite jarring when you're just beginning to come out of months of intensity. The good news is it's generally short-lived with your new found equilibrium returning once the anniversary has passed.

Resolution does not mean you will never feel the loss ever again. From time to time, you will feel a renewed sense of grief for the person you lost. Sometimes the anniversary of the death many years later will trigger it. Sometimes a special event like a wedding or the birth of a grandchild that they're not here to see will trigger it. Sometime it gets triggered for no apparent reason. It's just there for an instant, and then it's gone.

A Note about Elisabeth Kübler-Ross and the 5 Stages of Grief

Elizabeth Kübler-Ross made a great contribution to our understanding of grief. Unfortunately that contribution has been largely misunderstood.

In her early work, Kübler-Ross delineated 5 stages of grief; denial, anger, bargaining, depression and acceptance, as they applied to people diagnosed with cancer.

These descriptions can be useful in understanding what is going on when you're in one of these states, but to think of these as stages as a linear progression does a huge disservice to those who are grieving.

Normal grief is much messier than that. In normal grief, you may experience these 'stages' many times, sometimes simultaneously, and with a rapidity that can leave you breathless.

So although you will undoubtedly experience all of these 'stages' during your grieving process, you will experience them hundreds of times and in an unordered, chaotic fashion.

It's not uncommon to feel like you have made progress, only to get thrown back into tumult as if the loss just happened. Anniversaries, holidays and birthdays are the frequent catalysts for renewed grief, but it can happen at any time in response to just about anything or nothing at all.

Although Kübler-Ross's version seems to wrap grief up nicely for our minds to grasp, it does a great disservice to expect your grief to be that tidy. It's just not. Most grief is a tangled mess of emotion, and that's exactly how it's supposed to be.

PERFECTLY NORMAL AND NATURAL RESPONSES TO GRIEF

If I can impart one piece of wisdom to you in this book, it is this...let your grief be the guide and follow it where it takes you.

As messy and out of control as grieving can be, there is an inner wisdom that only becomes apparent after the fact. If this is your first major loss or a particularly profound loss, you'll have to take my word for it...I know it doesn't feel that way right now.

People often wonder if they're grieving is normal, if they're doing it right...you are perfectly normal if your emotions are constantly moving and you're totally exhausted at the end of the day. The key is...if it's moving, you're on track.

When in the midst of grief, it often feels like you're drowning and will never resurface. I promise, it's not true, it just feels that way. In time, the intensity diminishes and you find ways of moving on.

The following list is hardly exhaustive, but these are some of the most common reactions, experiences, and questions people report especially in the first few months following a death.

They are not offered in any particular order because that's how they appear...a hodge podge of emotions and experiences. In the moment they can feel like they will never end but they do...all of them are generally short lived and just part of the process.

- Feeling Numb

- Finding It Hard to Believe That the Death has Really Happened

- Physical Pain

- Feeling Physically Sick

- Changes in Appetite

- Increased Use of Alcohol and Drugs

- Increased Tobacco Use

- Feeling The Need for Prescription Medication

- Feeling Restless and Fidgety

- Needing to be in Constant Motion

- Trouble Concentrating

- Being Accident Prone

- Difficulty Completing Tasks

- Trouble Sleeping

- Dreams

- Reliving the Death

- Fear about Your Own Health and Well Being

- Developing Symptoms Similar to Those of the Person Who Died

- Visiting the Cemetery (or Not)

- Feeling Exhausted

- Feeling Renewed Grief around Birthdays, Holidays, Anniversaries, and Other Special Occasions

- Telling and Retelling Stories about the Person and/or the Death

- Talking To the Person Who Died

- Thinking You Hear, Smell, See or Feel Them

- Volatile Mood Changes

- Anger

- Unusual Irritability

- Indecisiveness

- Preoccupation With the Person Who Died

- Acting or Speaking Like the Person Who Died

- Losing Your Sense of Purpose and Direction

- Isolation and Loneliness

- Feeling Sorry for Yourself

- Not Feeling Needed

- Tears

- No Tears

- Relief

- Feeling Like You're Going Crazy

- Difficulty Getting Along with Your Family

- Being Afraid You'll Forget Them

- Insensitive Comments from Others

- People Worrying about You

- Pressure to Move On

- Living in the Past

- You Can't Remember Anything Bad about the Person...or Anything Good

- Feeling Overwhelmed

- Money /Changes in Spending Habits

- Sadness and Depression

- A Crisis in Faith / Changes in Your Religious or Spiritual Practice

- Guilt

- Having Trouble Remembering What They Looked Like or Sounded Like

Feeling Numb

Soon after a death, it's common for people to report feeling numb. Sometimes people will be surprised that they aren't crying or really feeling the loss as they think they should.

This is certainly something that can make you question whether your experience is normal. After all, how is it that someone you love has just died and you can't feel it? You know intellectually he or she died, but you feel numb.

Nothing's wrong with you. In fact, everything is working perfectly...your psyche is taking very good care of you. Just like when the body goes into shock following a physical injury, so the mind and emotions go into shock when someone dies.

This is a protective and healing mechanism which allows you to take in the magnitude of what has happened slowly. Truthfully, our nervous systems are not equipped to take in this kind of trauma all at once, so we're protected in a way that lets it filter in a bit at a time.

It can take 3 to 6 months for the death to become real and the numbness to wear off. By then, you are better prepared to deal with the full reality of your loss without being totally decimated by it. That's not to say it's easy, but you will be in a stronger position to deal with your feelings 3 to 6 months after the death than immediately following it.

The key throughout this process is to trust the grief and to follow where it leads. Over time, you will begin to notice the numbness fading. As long as your grief keeps changing over time (months), you can be pretty sure you're on track.

When to Get Help

I would recommend getting help...support group, clergy, grief counselor if you feel just as numb 3-6 months into your grief as you did immediately following the death.

Finding It Hard to Believe the Death Has Really Happened

Related to feeling numb, this response is more a response of the mind.

In the beginning, our mind simply cannot take in the full reality of our loss, so even though you know the person has died, you'll have moments of forgetfulness. You expect them to walk through the door after work or you pick up the phone to call them and for that split second, you forget...then you remember they're not there and they won't be walking through the door.

It's disconcerting for sure, and can feel like they've died all over again, but it's completely normal. This happens to almost everyone...less perhaps after very long illnesses, but even then it happens. You are so used to the person being there because they've been there for so long that it's really impossible to shift that quickly. Death may happen in a heartbeat, but it takes those of us left behind quite a while to catch up.

When to Get Help

Honestly, I'm not sure anyone really needs to get help with this one. It really is that typical in the first few months. If it's troublesome to you, join a support group because the people there will know exactly what you're experiencing and support you through it.

Physical Pain

Grief hurts...emotionally, mentally, and physically.

Although you expect emotional pain, feeling tightness and heaviness in the throat, in the chest, or in the pit of one's stomach often comes as a surprise. Back pain, too, can be related to your grief.

Often, the usual remedies don't work very well on this kind of pain. Nor is this the kind to be concerned about. Over time it passes.

It may take a while for this kind of pain to go away. The best thing you can do is stay with your grief and let it guide you.

Since we tend to tense our muscles in response to pain of all kinds...try breathing into the pain or around it to release the physical tension. This may release emotions you've been holding at bay and alleviate some of the physical pain. Because the tension is often the result of trying to protect ourselves from the emotional pain, it's important to be gentle with yourself.

When to Get Help

Get it checked out by a doctor if the pain concerns you or you think it may be something more serious. If there's no physical explanation for your pain and it doesn't improve over time (6+ months), you might want to talk with a counselor or join a support group. Chances are, emotional support is what's needed, but it can't hurt to get a more thorough physical as well. Don't let anyone discount your physical pain just because you're grieving.

Feeling Physically Sick

People who are grieving visit the doctor much more frequently than people who are not, with a multitude of physical complaints. Colds, back pain, chest pain, and a feeling of general malaise can all be directly related to your grief.

Although some complaints may be psychosomatic (making emotional pain physical, like the physical pain described above), others are less direct but equally real. Grief does impair the immune system like any other stressor. This is generally not serious, but it does mean you're more susceptible to anything that's going around.

The best thing you can do is to take very good care of yourself. That means doing the best you can to eat well, get enough sleep, and take plenty of time off. This is admittedly a challenge because eating well, getting enough sleep, and taking time off may be very hard to do right now. Be gentle with yourself and do the best you can.

When to Get Help

Any symptom that concerns you should be checked out by a doctor. It's probably nothing serious, but better safe than sorry. Conversely, don't let your symptoms be discounted as grief if you really believe there's something wrong.

Changes in Appetite

Eating more or less than usual is a common reaction. You may experience a complete loss of appetite or be ravenous all the time.

Grief is stressful. Most of us respond to stress with some sort of change in appetite. This is not the time to go on a diet. It is a time to take good care of yourself by eating as well as you can.

Over time, your appetite will return to normal. The only thing to do is do your best to eat well...regularly and healthfully...and over time, your appetite will return to normal.

When to Get Help

Although normal to gain or lose weight during this time, get some help if the changes in eating patterns persist for many months or your weight changes significantly. Though 10 - 20 pounds is probably normal, more than that may not be. Talk to your doctor and get support from a grief counselor or support group.

Increased Use of Alcohol and Drugs

Disclaimer: For those known to have problems with alcohol and drugs, don't go here...but you already know that right? Grief following a death is not an excuse to use.

For the rest of you, an increase in the occasional use of alcohol is pretty normal.

Honestly, sometimes the only healthy response to grief is to tie one on. I did the day I planned my mother's funeral. Taking an occasional respite from the extraordinary pain you're experiencing, is perfectly appropriate.

On the other hand, getting lost in the fog of abuse doesn't help either. For some, this can be a slippery slope that prolongs the grief rather than relieving it. When drinking or drugs become a means of avoiding your grief, you end up increasing your suffering. Eventually, the grief will break through. It could be days, weeks, or even years, but sooner or later, it will catch up.

Grief hurts. It takes courage to grieve, to let this process unfold naturally, but it is also the surest and quickest way through the pain. So take a respite here and there if you must (and you will), but don't let it sap your courage and sabotage the process.

When to Get Help

The good news is, if you're concerned about your substance

use, chances are it's not a problem, but it might be time to get some support for your grief; a support group, counselor or clergy person will probably be exactly what you need.

If you can't stop, it's time to get help - period. There's no time like the present. A local AA group would be the choice. Recovering alcoholics know lots about grief and can be very helpful in addressing both the substance and the grief.

Increased Tobacco Use

You're under stress, and if you're a smoker, your smoking will undoubtedly increase. This is not the time to quit. Grief is hard enough without setting yourself up to fail with this one. Even if the death was caused by lung cancer, this isn't the time to quit. This time next year would be the perfect time.

If you're a former smoker, you may be tempted to pick up a cigarette. Please don't. Wasn't quitting once enough? There are other ways of dealing with your stress. This one will only cause more misery in the end.

When to Get Help

Not much to do around this one other than join a support group.

Feeling The Need for
Prescription Medication

You may feel the need for tranquilizers, anti-anxiety medication, anti-depressants, or sleep aids, just to get through the day, and your doctor may be willing to prescribe them.

Short term use can be helpful if you're having a particularly hard time...not sleeping, not eating or you're unable to function at all, but they are not a panacea.

Grief is not a mood disorder like anxiety disorders and clinical depression, and it's certainly not an illness. It is a normal, natural and healthy response to a traumatic loss, so medication is of limited value and may actually prolong the process.

Medication is never recommended for long term use as a response to grief and should only be used for really extreme symptoms and then only for as long as you need to get the symptoms under control.

So, don't be concerned if you need medication to get a good night's sleep when you haven't slept in days, but don't rely on it to get you through the next year.

Obviously, don't take medications prescribed for something else or for someone else. Please check with your doctor first.

When to Get Help

If you have a pre-existing depression or anxiety disorder, continue under your doctor's care.

If you're not sleeping at all (really and truly not at all for days on end), talk to your doctor. At some point, the lack of sleep makes you less able to cope with all of the feelings you're experiencing, so taking something to help you sleep is perfectly appropriate.

Same goes for new symptoms of depression that persist without let up...sleeping all the time, not eating at all, staying in bed for days or weeks at a time, unrelenting tears. Persistent anxiety and panic attacks may also call for a short term medical intervention.

For most of you, a support group will do more than any amount of medication. I know I sound like a broken record and I also know how few of you will actually take this advice (that's why I wrote the book) but I have to say, support groups are the most effective help you can get...even better than this book.

A Warning: Many physicians are willing to prescribe these medications without adequate assessment. Some will even prescribe them to ease their own feelings of helplessness and discomfort in the face of your grief. Remember you are the ultimate authority about what you need, so don't be talked into using something you really don't need or don't feel comfortable with.

Feeling Restless and Fidgety

Grief is unsettling to say the least, and you may find there will be times when you don't know quite what to do with yourself...roaming around the house without any sense of direction or purpose.

Given the assault of emotions and the typical inability to concentrate, it makes sense that you might find yourself moving around a lot, moving from one activity to another, starting things only to leave them half done. This is not a character flaw. It's grief.

Rarely is this anything to be concerned about. Over time it will pass.

When to Get Help

If this happens in conjunction with other ongoing or extreme symptoms of anxiety, being assessed by a mental health professional would make sense.

Otherwise, you got it - a support group is your best resource.

Needing to be in Constant Motion

Some people have a need for frenetic activity. Just keeping busy can keep you from dwelling on your loss. This is fine for a time, but most people find they can't keep it up forever.

The key here is to let it be whatever it needs to be. If you need to stay busy, so be it.

Remember, grief is very wise and knows exactly what you need. Your job is to follow. If you need to stay busy, then that's what you need to do. When you need to stop, you'll know when it's time to do that as well.

As with all of these responses, quell your judgments and just let it be what it is - a normal and natural response to a profound loss.

It does get easier and less frenetic over time...it really does. I know it doesn't feel like it right now, but it does.

When to Get Help

The only time any professional intervention might be needed is if there is a pre-existing diagnosis of a bipolar disorder. Since most of you reading this book do not have that, there's nothing whatsoever to worry about...go to a group.

Trouble Concentrating

This is one of the most common responses to grief.

Let's face it, all of your attention is focused on your loss, making it very difficult to concentrate on anything else. It will pass.

One of the most commonly reported examples is not being able to read...reading the same paragraph over and over without any comprehension.

When to Get Help

If it's helpful to you, talk with a trusted friend, clergy, or support group.

Being Accident Prone

Grief can be all-consuming and totally distracting.

It can be really hard to pay attention to anything else...certainly not your daily routines. A lot of the time, you may feel like you're running on autopilot, which means you're not paying full attention to what you're doing.

This distractibility, combined with the lack of restful sleep can make you accident prone. This can be as simple, and annoying, as constantly dropping things, to as serious as falling and car accidents.

Once again, this is a time to take particularly good care of yourself. Try not to expect too much of yourself as in trying to accomplish more than you can really handle right now. Easy does it.

If you need help, ask for it. Asking someone to drive you to the store instead of driving yourself when you're distracted is a very good idea. Besides, the company might do you good, and it will make your friend feel useful (many of the people around you want to help but don't know how).

When to Get Help

Aside from the obvious medical intervention if you injure yourself, none is required.

Difficulty Completing Tasks

Given the lack of energy, the inability to concentrate, poor quality sleep, is it any wonder finishing things might be a problem? Besides, none of the usual day-to-day activities seem to matter much, right?

If there's something urgent that really has to get done, ask someone to do it for you or have someone come in to do it with you. Just having someone keep you company while you do it can help tremendously.

Whoever thought it was a good idea to deal with finances, wills and probate immediately after a death was out of their mind. What are they thinking? For these things, hire an accountant and lawyer. That's what they're there for and they really do relieve the burden.

When to Get Help

If it's not getting done and it matters (most of it doesn't), hire someone to do it for you. If you don't want to hire someone, have a friend come help you do it, or at least keep you company while you tackle it.

Trouble Sleeping

Almost everyone has trouble sleeping when they're grieving. Some of the most common sleep problems include...

• Having trouble getting to sleep.

• Waking in the middle of the night.

• Fitful sleep...more dozing than sleeping.

• Waking up unusually early and not being able to get back to sleep.

• Disturbing dreams.

• Sleeping through the night only to wake up exhausted.

• Lying awake at night and napping during the day.

These are all perfectly normal experiences for people who are grieving a loss. You may experience one or all of these in the first months (up to a year) following a death.

Being awake when the rest of the world's asleep with no one to talk to can feel horrible. I'd say there's a good chance you bought this book at 3 a.m. for that very reason. I was thinking about you as I was writing it.

Be gentle with yourself. Remember lying down and resting is good for you even if you can't sleep. Even the dozing on and off is better than nothing.

The worst thing you can do is try hard to sleep or beat yourself up for having trouble sleeping. That response is virtually guaranteed to keep you awake.

If lying in bed wide awake is too hard, I recommend getting up and doing something. Cleaning the house at 3 a.m. may seem odd, but why not? Doing something other than focusing on your grief and the lack of sleep can break the thought pattern that's keeping you awake.

You can also write, meditate, make art, look at photo albums, read, respond to email, write thank you notes, etc.

Trouble sleeping is just a normal part of the process. Grief hurts, and just like physical injuries, it takes time to heal. Restful sleep will return in time.

When to Get Help

Consult your doctor if you're not sleeping at all. Taking a mild sleep aid may help in the short term, but this is not a long-term solution. For the vast majority of people, sleep returns as you begin to heal.

Dreams

In those times when you do sleep, you may find yourself dreaming about the person who died. For many, this is welcome remembrance, and for others, it's not. Dreams are the way our minds process life experiences and they are a normal part of healing. The content and emotions associated with your dreams will change over time as you move through your grief.

Not dreaming about the person who died is also a common experience. Not dreaming about them can be disturbing to many people. No dreams or no remembered dreams can be experienced as an additional loss when we look to them as a way of staying connected to the person who is gone.

You may go through periods of dreaming a lot and then not at all.

This is all perfectly normal. The only thing to do is to be with whatever's going on in the moment. There is no right way or wrong way when it comes to dreams or grief...there's just your way.

When to Get Help

Talking to a trusted friend or going to a support group is all that's called for here.

Reliving the Death

It's not at all uncommon to repeatedly replay the dying process in your mind...thinking about what happened, thinking about what might have happened, regretting what was said or not said, replaying particularly traumatic moments over and over.

This is all normal and is your way of making sense of what happened.

The images of death are memories with such emotional impact we may always have vivid memories, but the need to revisit it again and again passes with time, as does the intense emotional charge.

Telling the story of what happened is the most healing thing you can do. Sharing our personal stories is how we make meaning out of all our life experiences. This is especially true with the loss of someone we love, an experience that feels so meaningless.

Talking to a friend who's willing to listen can help tremendously, as can writing. Sometimes families can share their stories and sometimes they can't. (See *Difficulty Getting Along with Your Family*)

Over time, you'll notice the story changing, and eventually, you'll just get tired of telling it. This is a sign that you're successfully moving through your grief and beginning to reinvest in the future.

Don't try to force it. You will probably need to tell this story many, many, many times. Your friends may tire of hearing it. This is when support groups help the most. Other people who have experienced similar loses never seem to tire of listening.

When to Get Help

The only help that's needed here is someone to listen...friends, family, clergy, counselors, support groups.

Fear about Your Own Health and Well Being

Well that makes sense doesn't it? Being afraid you might get sick and die too...sure makes sense to me.

This is true whether your loss was caused by a prolonged illness, a sudden death, or an accident. You may find yourself worrying about getting the same disease to the point of developing similar symptoms. (See *Developing Symptoms Similar to Those of the Person Who Died*).

If your loss was caused by an accident, you may fear being in the same situation or going to the place where it happened. It's not uncommon for people to go miles out of their way to avoid the scene of an accident.

The best thing you can do is to simply acknowledge what you're experiencing.

When to Get Help

Go to the doctor if you have any health concerns. It's likely there's nothing wrong, but this will help to relieve your mind.

Developing Symptoms
Similar to Those of the Person Who Died

This is similar to psychology and medical students thinking they have every disorder they study.

If this loss involved a lengthy illness, you've been focused on that illness and all its symptoms for some time. Now that the person has died, you may find yourself experiencing similar symptoms just because all of those details are still on your mind.

For any death from an illness, prolonged or sudden, taking on the symptoms of the person who died can also be a way of processing what has happened.

The key is to recognize what it is and let it take you where you need to go. This is the wisdom of grief at work, giving you a physical means for making sense out of what has happened.

When to Get Help

Go to the doctor if you have any health concerns. Better safe than sorry, but most of this is just your grief taking physical form for a short period of time.

Visiting the Cemetery (or Not)

Many people get tremendous comfort from visiting the grave.

If it brings you comfort, by all means go. Visiting the cemetery, bringing flowers, and talking to the person who died are very common forms of comfort. Some people have been known to visit the cemetery regularly for many years following a death. Others feel drawn to visit on birthdays, anniversaries, or holidays.

Then there are those who never want to go back ever again. This can be because it brings on too much discomfort, but it can also be because you don't feel any greater connection to the person there than you do anywhere else. Sometimes the greater comfort may come from visiting a place you shared together.

There is no right or wrong here. The only criteria is whether it brings comfort to you...or not. Forcing the issue either way does you a disservice for no good reason. Do what feels best for you even when it's different from what other family members choose. (See *Difficulty Getting Along with Your Family*).

When to Get Help

If you're forcing the issue either way, pushing yourself to visit when you don't really want to, or avoiding it when you'd really like to visit, seeking help from the clergy or a support group might be helpful.

Feeling Exhausted

Grief takes a phenomenal amount of emotional energy. At times, it will take ALL of your emotional energy. You can sit in a chair all day long and feel like you've run a marathon by the end of it. Truth is, you have run a marathon, a mental and emotional marathon, and it's one you'll run again tomorrow.

When you combine this expenditure of mental and emotional energy with difficulty sleeping, is it any wonder you're feeling exhausted? Rest will help, but even if you're sleeping, you may wake up feeling exhausted. It's just the nature of the process.

As you begin to heal, your grief will cease to consume all of your energy, and your exhaustion will begin to diminish. In the meantime, be gentle with yourself, take as much time off as you need, and nap when you can. Understand that you're just not going to have the energy to do all that you would normally do, and let that be okay. Feeling exhausted is a temporary state we all seem to go through. It passes as we begin to heal.

When to Get Help

See your doctor if you're not sleeping at all...and I mean at all...or if you think this might be related to another physical problem. Exhaustion can be a symptom of other things, but chances are, your current exhaustion is simply because you're expending a tremendous amount of emotional and mental energy on your grief.

Feeling Renewed Grief Around Birthdays, Holidays, Anniversaries, and Other Special Occasions

With every birthday, holiday, and family event, we are hit again with the magnitude of our loss. Although it can be quite intense, it's generally short lived. Even years later, we may find ourselves feeling unaccountably sad, only to realize it's the anniversary of a death.

The 'firsts' are the worst. The first birthday, the first anniversary, the first Thanksgiving and Christmas can feel like tremendous obstacles when you're anticipating them. They are hard, no question about it, but often the anticipation is worse than the reality.

Special events are a powerful reminder of your loss. With each event, you may be thrown back into feelings you thought were easing. This is absolutely normal, and the recurrence of intense grief is generally short lived.

Each individual and family needs to decide for themselves what to do with family traditions. Some feel best continuing traditions to the letter, while others want to do something completely different. There's no right or wrong here...just your way.

Some find it helpful to create a special ritual to acknowledge and include the person who has died. This can be as simple as lighting a special candle, going to the cemetery, having a special memorial service, volunteering at a soup kitchen, reading a favorite poem, or looking at family movies together. You are limited only by your imagination. It doesn't have to be a big thing.

It's not unusual for family members to disagree about what to do for a holiday or special occasion. (See *Difficulty Getting Along with Your Family*). This is one of the few times I would encourage you to compromise because it's generally better to be together than apart, even when it's not exactly the way you would have wanted it.

One of the dangers here is that it's easy to assume you're going to celebrate one way, when other family members may be making very different assumptions. A great deal of conflict can be eliminated by planning ahead and including everyone in the conversation.

Although the intensity diminishes, special occasions can trigger renewed grief for years following a death. It's not uncommon for people to report feeling down or crying for no apparent reason only to realize it's the anniversary of a death that happened years ago.

When to Get Help

The only support I'd recommend is the usual support group. Some bereavement programs offer special groups for surviving the holidays. These can be quite helpful.
If family conflicts seem insurmountable, having your clergy or a family counselor facilitate the conversation would

probably be helpful.

Telling and Retelling Stories about the Person and/or the Death

The telling and retelling of stories is how we make meaning out of the person's life and death. It's really that simple.

Your friends might call it ruminating, but it's perfectly normal. It actually goes way beyond normal - it's essential. Talking about the person you love, talking about their illness and their death is an integral part of the healing process.

On the surface, it can appear like you're obsessing, but in reality, the repetitive storytelling is the means through which you make the death real, remember the person, make meaning of their life and death, make meaning of your relationship with them, and figure out how you will remain in relationship with them as you move forward without them.

At one level, it's a way of staying connected. At another, it's a way of making sense out of your entire relationship with this person, including their death. Stories are a potent vehicle we all use to create a bridge from a life that included the physical presence of the person to a full and meaningful life without them.

Over time, the story subtly changes from a focus on the death and grief to a new focus on remembrance. One of the most significant shifts is that the story becomes more real. The person is no longer idealized but is remembered as the real human being they were. (See *You Can't Remember Anything Bad about the Person...or Anything Good*).

The problem with this kind of storytelling is that your friends may tire of listening long before you tire of telling. Even with lots of friends who are willing to listen, the stories in time may wear out their welcome. This is another place where support groups can really help, and because people in support groups are so attuned to the issues, they will often pick up on the subtle shifts before you or anyone else realize they're happening.

When friends start getting bored, it may be time to find new audiences. Support groups are only one choice. Talking with your clergy, talking to a grief counselor, reaching out to the newly bereaved (you need to be ready to listen as well), and writing are all ways you can continue to tell your story.

Over time, you won't have the need to tell it. Not only will the story have shift in focus, but it will also start getting shorter with less detail and less emotional charge. These are signs that you are healing.

The most important thing is - DON'T LET ANYONE SHUT YOU UP until you're ready.

When to Get Help

The help that's really needed here are people willing to listen. If people aren't available, then write it.

If the story remains unchanged over time, you might want to talk with a counselor who specializes in grief. Sometimes, the story really hasn't changed, in which case, a counselor can help your grief get moving again. More frequently, the story really is changing, you just haven't noticed it yet. A counselor can mirror that back to you when no one else is.

Talking To the Person Who Died

Some might call it crazy...but only if they haven't lost someone close to them.

Why wouldn't you talk to them? It's generally comforting and who's to say they're not listening...nobody really knows for sure. What I do know is that I have personally found comfort in it, as have the vast majority of people I've counseled.

When to Get Help

Unless there's a pre-existing psychiatric disorder where this might be indicative of something more serious, there is no help needed other than the usual support groups, clergy, grief counselors, and trusted friends.

Thinking You Hear, Smell, See, or Feel Them

Some people find this comforting and others find it disconcerting in the extreme, but it happens to almost everyone at some point...you see them standing in the doorway, you hear their voice whispering in your ear, or you walk into a room and get a whiff of their perfume or after shave. Sometimes, you just feel their presence.

You are definitely not going crazy. You are not hallucinating. You're not dreaming. Personally, I don't even believe it's a kind wish fulfillment, but rather a real physical reminder of the love you shared. It's a memory, not wish fulfillment, and it happens all the time.

Over time, the frequency of these experiences diminish, but you may experience occasional moments far into the future.

When to Get Help

All the usual here...support groups, clergy, grief counselors, and trusted friends. There's nothing unusual here and certainly nothing that requires any kind of intervention or anything that's going to push you over the edge. It's that normal.

The only concern here is if there is a pre-existing psychiatric disorder, but then you're already under a doctor's care, right?

Volatile Mood Changes

Grief is a rocky road. Some say it feels like a roller coaster where emotions rise and fall with frightening speed and diversity. These mood swings can be sparked by little things or nothing at all and can be quite disconcerting because they come out of the blue without warning.

It is not uncommon for people to burst into tears, feel a rage totally out of synch with what's going on in the moment, or to experience intense anxiety for no reason at all. Frequently, you will find yourself cycling through these with additional periods where you feel pretty 'normal' only to be hit again by a wave of intense emotion.

The emotional roller coaster of grief is a response to a profound life-changing event, and because we feel so shattered by it, we have little left to moderate all of the feelings that emerge. Accepting that you can't control them and that they're a normal part of the process generally helps.

As long as it keeps moving, it's normal. Normal grief is all over the place.

On the surface, there appears to be no rhyme or reason to these intense emotional swings, but from sitting with hundreds of people who are grieving, I've learned to trust the process. Whether you're consciously aware of it or not, you are continually processing what has happened, and it frequently breaks through to surface without warning.

Over time, your feelings become less volatile and more consistent. In other words, as your grief progresses, you heal and very gradually, you begin to create a life with a present, future, and a past that has founds its' place.

When to Get Help

First, give it some time. If you feel after several months (at least 6-9 months) the volatile moods haven't changed at all, then you might want to check in with a grief counselor, but for the vast majority, the volatility and intensity will vary and eventually diminish.

Anger

Anger takes many forms; anger they died, anger they left you, anger at the doctors who didn't save them, anger at God, anger about what you're left to deal with, anger at other family members for what they did and didn't do, and on and on it goes. There's usually plenty of anger to go around.

All of this anger is perfectly understandable and normal.

Anger is just part of the process of grieving. Anger denied turns into depression, so it's really important to acknowledge it. It's okay to be angry they left you. It's okay to be angry with God. It's fine to be angry at the doctors.

Most importantly, it's okay to be angry at the person who died. Maybe you're angry because they got sick and died. Maybe you're angry they didn't go to the doctor sooner. Maybe you're angry they left you with a financial mess. Whatever the reason, it's okay. Just because they died doesn't mean you shouldn't be angry at them.

You may also experience anger in response to feeling so out of control of what has happened to you. There are very few life events as out of our control as death, so some anger in response to it is to be expected.

Over time, the anger resolves. You may feel it off and on for a while, but over time, it does resolve.

The most useful thing you can do with it is to acknowledge it. Talking about it is certainly effective, but not everyone is comfortable talking, so even if you choose not to talk about it, please don't pretend you're not angry when you really are. In addition to talking, writing and making art can be very effective ways of expressing and working through your anger.

Anger makes most people very uncomfortable, almost as uncomfortable as death, so it's not uncommon for friends and family to try to stop it, talk you out of it, and make you feel like you're wrong for being angry. You're not. As long as you're not hurting anyone, don't worry about it.

And don't let anyone (including yourself) try to force you into forgiveness before you're good and ready. Forgiveness is a good thing and comes in time, but when you force yourself to forgive while you're still feeling angry, it's not real forgiveness. It also tends to backfire with anger erupting unexpectedly later on. Better to feel it, move through it and let the forgiveness come in its' own time.

A note about being angry at other family members.

Anger at other family members is often rooted in feeling that your family isn't really there for you and they probably aren't there for you in the way you'd like.

During most life events, we turn to our families for support, but when there is a shared loss, your family members don't have any more emotional reserves than you do so there's not a lot available for you.

Each of you are grieving differently and may be feeling different things at different times. If you're feeling angry and they're not in that moment, they probably can't support you in it. This can feel like another loss and it is, but it's a just temporary one. This is the time to reach out to support groups, clergy, and friends. (See *Difficulty Getting Along with Your Family*).

When to Get Help

Normally, friends, clergy, and support groups are enough to deal with this kind of anger.

You should seek counseling if your anger feels out of control, is being expressed physically, or is unrelenting over weeks or months.

If your anger is rooted in the fact that you had a difficult relationship with this person long before they died, counseling is recommended. In this case, much of your anger may be about the relationship you had or didn't have with the person, and that complicates your grief.

Unusual Irritability

Yes, the death of someone you love can certainly make you feel just a tad irritable.

Irritability is often an expression of suppressed anger. See section above on anger. It can also stem from feeling overwhelmed or just plain tired.

It's normal and relatively short lived.

Irritability often gets directed at whatever or whoever crosses our path. As much as you may think it's the immediate situation, it's important to realize that it's more likely to be your frustration and grief that's at the root of your irritability.

When to Get Help

Chronic and habitual irritability can be a sign of depression, especially if it's out of character for you. If it goes on for weeks or months without relief, it would be a good idea to talk with a counselor.

Indecisiveness

Making decisions can be difficult following the death of someone you love. The ground underneath you has been profoundly shaken. Your way of being in the world has been shattered. Normal isn't normal anymore, and all of the criteria you have used to make decisions in the past may seem irrelevant or simply don't apply to the present situation.

Even if you're used to making decisions on your own, you may become indecisive for a time. If you lost the person you're used to making decisions with, it's that much harder. Now, you have to trust yourself to make decisions you used to share. The self-doubt inherent in that can be enough to make anyone indecisive.

The first year following a death is largely about finding a new normal. The old normal doesn't exist anymore. Making decisions when you have no idea what life is going to look like tomorrow, never mind next year, makes them very hard to make, and it's probably not a good idea to even try if you can possibly avoid it.

In most cases, you're too disoriented to be making big life-changing decisions right now anyway, so a bit of indecisiveness is probably a good thing. It will keep you from doing anything rash. A good rule of thumb is to avoid making any big decisions, like moving, for at least a year. Even if you're not having trouble making decisions, your emotions during the first year following a death are so volatile that you may find you want something very different 12 months from now.

Sometimes, your indecisiveness will be about things that just don't seem very important right now...who cares what you have for dinner?

Other times, whether you're actually able to make a decision or not, small decisions...what to wear, what to eat, what color to choose...take on monumental proportions. They feel more important than they actually are. This is a wonderful coping strategy. If you focus on the small stuff, you won't have to think about the big stuff.

Unless your indecisiveness becomes chronic, there's nothing to worry about.

It's okay to let other people make decisions about things that need immediate action and to defer other decisions until you're really ready to make them.

Do not let anyone force you into making a decision you're not ready to make, especially within the first year following a death.

When to Get Help

The usual support group, clergy and friends are all helpful.

If your indecisiveness becomes chronic, does not resolve after the first year, and it's out of character for you, meeting with a counselor might be appropriate.

Indecisiveness can also be a symptom of depression, but you can't make that assumption because it can just as easily be plain old grief. A counselor who specializes in grief can help you sort it out.

Preoccupation With the Person Who Died

Thinking about the person who died is normal, even when that's all you're thinking about.

Even though you loved them very much and your life may have been centered around them, you will probably find that you're thinking about them more than when they were alive. This is all perfectly normal.

It may last for many months. Then somewhere down the line, you'll notice you're starting to think about other things. It may be for just a brief moment. It may be so subtle you don't even notice it at first, but it is a sign you're beginning to heal. Sometimes you may be startled to realize you just spent a few moments thinking about something else, only to return to thoughts about the person you love.

Most people find these thoughts comforting, but some find them disturbing, especially if they're interfering with work or daily life. Honestly, all you can do is go with it. There's nothing to be fixed here.

It's to remember that you can't force these thoughts to stop, even if you wanted to. When you're ready, you'll start thinking about other things and the total preoccupation will end, but only when you're really ready.

Pay attention to whether your thoughts about the person are changing over time. Typically, the constant barrage of thoughts will diminish and the content will change. This is the real indicator that you're moving in the right direction.

An example...immediately following the death, you may be able to think of nothing other than the illness, the death, and the funeral. Over time, your thoughts become more about the person than their illness or death. Even though you may still be thinking about them all the time, the content of your thoughts is changing. The frequency will follow.

The only time to be concerned about this is if continues over months without let up or any kind of change...in frequency and/or content. Otherwise, it's normal, and don't let anyone tell you it isn't.

Again the people around you may be very uncomfortable with this and encourage you to stop living in the past. You need to understand that comments like that are an expression of their own discomfort and have nothing to do with you.

When to Get Help

If you're still preoccupied in an all-consuming way with thoughts about the person who died and the content and/or frequency hasn't changed, and you're still thinking about them 24/7 as you move into the second year, you might want to talk with someone. Remember, normal grief is fluid and volatile, so any one thought or emotion that doesn't change over time, is worth looking at.

Often a support group is enough to help you. Other times,

you might want to talk to someone in the clergy or a grief counselor.

Acting or Speaking Like the Person Who Died

This is an unconscious phenomenon, but it's not at all uncommon to take on the characteristics, mannerisms or speech patterns of the person you lost.

It's just one way you may process the loss, and that's not a bad thing. Rather than talking about them or thinking about them, you may just become like them in some way. Generally, this is a temporary phenomenon and other times, we really do take on characteristics of the person who died. Maybe it's a way of keeping them with us. Maybe it's because we want to emulate what we liked about them.

In my experience, children who lack the words to talk about their grief or who lack the emotional understanding to grasp death (under age 7), may be more likely to take on the personality traits of the person who died.

That's not to say anything about your emotional maturity. Anyone of any age may do this. It's just that this coping mechanism is accessible to a wider range of individuals.

When to Get Help

This is totally normal. If it bothers you in yourself or someone else, you can find support in a grief support group.

Losing Your Sense of Purpose and Direction

Think about it...life was going along just fine, you had plans for the future, those plans involved the person who has died. Then all of a sudden, there's a life-threatening illness or an accident and this person who was so much a part of your life is gone.

Truth is, you're starting over, so all of the old hopes and dreams and plans are up for revaluation. Your life has irrevocably changed and it can be really hard to discover a renewed sense of purpose and direction.

This is so very normal and resolves over time. Give yourself the time and space you need for your new life to emerge. You don't need to force this or judge it or any of that...just let it unfold for a while.

As time goes on, you may find this experience to be an opportunity, bittersweet though it may be, in which you find new purpose in life or you choose to take a different path than the one you were on. This is one of those silver lining gifts we rarely grasp while sitting in the middle of all that pain, but that doesn't mean it's not there. Usually these gifts only become clear in retrospect, and though thankful for the gift, the price always seems too high.

When to Get Help

I know I've said it before...support groups are your best option.

If you're still adrift beyond the first year and your grief feels like it's stagnating into a chronic condition, then you might want to talk to your clergy or a grief counselor.

Isolation and Loneliness

Ah, you can't be with them and you can be without them...them being the people around you.

It is not at all uncommon to feel unbearably lonely following a death, particularly if you lost a spouse, best friend or child. The loss of anyone who was part of your day to day life can trigger a loneliness that no one else can fill.

As a result, you may want to isolate yourself by withdrawing from your usual family and social life. Sometimes, it's just easier to be alone than lonely around other people.

Sometimes, people isolate themselves because no one seems to understand. Sometimes, it's because everyone else is going on with their lives while you're still living in a slow motion fog.

For a while, this is understandable. Isolating yourself for months on end is not. As much as you may be feeling out of synch with the rest of life and feeling like it's just easier to be alone, it's not helpful over the long haul.

You need to be around other people, but not just anyone. This is a time for being very selective about the people you choose to spend time with. You do not need to spend time with the stupid people...you know the ones...they tell you you're better off...or they encourage you to get over it...or they're morbidly curious about details you don't want to share.

You also don't want to hang out with people who are afraid to talk about the person who died...the name is going to come up. If they keep changing the subject, this is not a helpful person for you right now.

All of this passes in time, but in the meantime, try to spend some time with a trusted friend who doesn't feel compelled to fix it, but who can be with you wherever you are in the moment, which includes not talking about it and going to a movie. They can be hard to come by, which is why I keep encouraging you to check out support groups - those people get it.

When to Get Help

A support group is absolutely the best possible thing you can do here. Period!

If your isolation becomes entrenched, talking with a grief counselor would probably be a good idea. Isolation can be a symptom of depression or it can just be a normal part of the grieving process. Making the call between the two can be difficult so get an outside opinion if you have any doubts at all. Either way, you will get the help you need or you'll relieve your mind from worry.

The only caveat is to make sure the professional you talk to is really an expert in grief. Anyone else is going to call it depression whether it is or not, and it's just as likely not.

Feeling Sorry for Yourself

Well why not? Unless it's five years down the line and you're still feeling sorry for yourself, you have every right in the world to feel sorry for yourself without guilt or remorse.

I've heard many people say they shouldn't feel sorry for themselves because they're not the one who died (or they still have a good life) but let's get this straight...being the one left behind is hard...terribly, terribly hard...and resenting it and feeling sorry for yourself just goes with the territory.

Again, as long as this doesn't become entrenched as a way of life, there is absolutely nothing to worry about. Honestly, I'd find it a little odd if you didn't have at least a little tiny bit of a twinge of self pity.

Don't listen to the people who try to talk you out of it or want to fix it. You need people around who can be with you without flinching, no matter what you're feeling.

Unless this is a life-long personality trait, a different issue entirely, this will pass with all the rest...in its' own time. Give yourself the gift of space and time to feel just what you're feeling. It really does go away faster that way.

When to Get Help

You know what to do, right? The usual support group, clergy

or trusted friend are all that's required.

Not Feeling Needed

When someone dies, we experience a multitude of secondary losses. Losing the feeling of being needed can be one of those.

We all need to feel needed. It's part of the human condition. It's one of the ways we find meaning in life and in our relationships with other people. If you experienced a sense of purpose in caring for the person who died, then their death may have set you adrift without anyone to care for, without anyone who needs your care. That's a tremendous loss.

Sometimes this loss is about the experience of caring for the person who died, especially if they died at home. Let's face it - if you were the primary caregiver for a loved one who had a long illness, your entire life revolved around taking care of them, and it probably went on for many months, if not years.

Exhausting and terrifying as it is, it's a privilege to take care of someone you love when they're sick and dying. There's a satisfaction in making sure they're not in pain, in being there when they need something in the middle of the night, or in being their advocate with the doctors and nurses. Not being needed like that anymore is a real loss.

Another facet of this is the assault to our very identity. Whether it was your job to mow the lawn, do the laundry, cook the meals or clean up after, whether you provided financial security or took care of the house, those activities had meaning because of who you did them for. Without that person to do those things for, the question becomes who are you without them?

The loss of someone we love challenges our concepts about who we are in the world, who needs us, and who's going to need us in the future. It challenges us to find new meaning and purpose in a life that is no longer entwined with someone else's.

The key here is to acknowledge the additional loss, and to focus on taking care of yourself. You need to be there for you right now. In time, your generosity of spirit will find others to care for, maybe not in the same way, but to care for nonetheless. In time, you will find useful and meaningful relationships and activities, but for now, the focus needs to be on healing your own heart.

What won't work is trying to plug someone else in too fast. Poking around in your grown children's lives because you need to have someone to care for is probably not going to go over well. Remarrying quickly can also be like stepping into quicksand. Take your time and focus your attention on yourself. It's not selfish. It will allow you, in time, to be genuinely needed and useful to others.

When to Get Help

Not much to do here other than the usual support group,

clergy or trusted friend. The best part of joining a support group is that you are needed by all the other group members. The sharing that goes on is very reciprocal.

Counseling can be helpful in sorting out the identity issues, but much of this resolves as you move through your grief. If you're feeling stuck around this issue or getting into difficult relationships with others as a result, that would be the time to get some help.

Tears

We all pretty much expect this one.

What we don't expect is how erratic and unpredictable they can be. It's possible to be walking down the street and burst into tears for no apparent reason. Something as insignificant as a traffic light turning can cause us to tear up. When we're grieving, tears can pop up for little reasons, big reasons, or no reason at all, and they're often gone as quickly as they came.

The real trick with tears is to let them be. Trying not to cry is probably the surest way I know of to end up in a full-blown crying binge. Not that there's anything wrong with that, but typically, the tears come and go rapidly with occasionally longer crying jags. All of it is completely normal.

In this as in all these responses to grief, grief knows the way. Your job is to follow. If you need cry, let it be.

When to Get Help

The usual things are all helpful, but the only time you really need to get some help is if you are crying all the time...every day, all day long without let up, especially if this continues for several days in a row.

I want to be perfectly clear here. I am <u>not</u> talking about feeling like the tears will never stop which is fairly common, but really never stopping. Normally, tears come and go, sometimes quite frequently, but there are spaces between the tears. When there are no spaces between the tears, it's time to get some help for this. I would recommend a counselor specializing in grief.

The other time to get help is if you have a history or a pre-existing diagnosis of depression. Just make sure your mental health professional really understands grief as well as they understand depression.

No Tears

Most people assume that grieving means tears, and it often does, but it is not at all uncommon for people to report never crying...and every one of them questions it. If this is you, don't worry about it. Tears are not a requirement for grieving successfully.

Some of the most common experiences are...

• Some people just don't cry...period. And you know what? It's all okay. However you need to grieve, with or without tears, is just fine.

• No tears may be due to a prolonged illness. It's possible to do much of your grieving during the illness. Although never entirely ready for a death, no matter how anticipated, it is possible to be ready enough for the tears to be well in the past.

• The issue may be about having watched a slow decline over many years as happens with Alzheimer's disease...the person was dying a little bit at a time and you were grieving a little bit at a time along with them. When experienced gradually, no single event may be enough to elicit tears, but you were grieving nonetheless.

• Often, people report feeling like they want to cry, but can't. Sometimes it's described as tension or heaviness in the chest with a longing for the relief tears would bring. It's an awful feeling, but it's quite common and totally normal.

Eventually, one of two things will happen...the tears will come or the tension releases without them. Some people have found watching sad movies or listening to music can help access the tears, but you really don't need to force it. The tears will come if and when you're ready for them.

• Some people try to block the tears, some more successfully than others, because they're afraid the tears will never stop once they start. All I can say is the tears do stop...really they do. If you need to cry, give yourself permission to do it. Blocked grief can backfire by turning into depression, creating more intense pain later, or making it difficult to move on.

Not crying does not necessarily mean blocked grief. If you're not crying, for whatever reason, chances are, you've found other normal responses on this list that you are experiencing. We all grieve differently, in our own unique way, and with our own unique set of responses. Your way is just your way. That goes for this experience just like all the rest.

When to Get Help

If you're still really concerned about it and I haven't put your mind to rest, talk to somebody...the usual support group, clergy or friends will probably be enough.

Relief

I think of this as death's dirty little secret. It seems so selfish somehow to experience a sense of relief when someone has died, but many people do and most never admit it.

Anyone who has been a caregiver to someone during a lengthy illness will undoubtedly feel some relief when it's finally over. Not because you wanted them to die, but because you're exhausted.

If you've been the primary caregiver who has been shouldering most of the responsibility for this person's care, chances are, you're tired beyond measure...not just from the emotional exertion of saying goodbye, but you've been the one running up and down the stairs, making sure they got their medications, running out to the drugstore or making sure somebody else did. You've changed the bed in the middle of the night. You've provided support on the way to the bathroom. You are physically and emotionally exhausted. Who wouldn't feel some relief about that being over?

Relief can also come from the certainty of a death that has finally occurred. Certainty is always easier to live with than uncertainty, even when the certainty of death is the last thing you want.

Sometimes the relief can be due to you having had a difficult relationship with the person who died. This can bring on all sorts of guilt. Some relationships are just so hard that we'd never be in them by choice. We're in them because it's family. And yes, sometimes we're glad it's over. Don't let this kind of relief twist you up. It's a normal, natural reaction when you had a difficult relationship with the person who died.

When to Get Help

There's little here that needs attention. In most cases, support groups are the best option. You will find other people there who have experienced relief. It never fails when someone brings it up, heads start nodding around the table.

If you had a difficult relationship with the person who died, I would recommend getting some counseling. Difficult relationships make grief harder because there's more going on than just the death. Though you may be feeling relief that the person is gone, all that history is still there and you still need some resolution.

Feeling Like You're Going Crazy

Without a doubt, this is the most common fear I hear from people who are grieving.

If it feels like you're going crazy, you're probably exactly where you need to be. As you look at this list of normal responses, many of them look like symptoms of something very serious, and they are. Grief is serious, but it's not a disease, and it's certainly not something in need of fixing.

In the case of grief, crazy is a sign of health because it speaks to the chaos of emotions that make up the normal grieving process. Part of what feels so crazy is the many and varied experiences we have and the rapid succession of feelings.

Not only is there a vast array of emotions, they're often contradictory. Many of the responses listed here look mighty contradictory when you try to hold them together logically. Grief is not logical, and trying to make it seem logical is an exercise in futility and frustration.

The surest and fastest way through is to follow the grief wherever it takes you, contradictions and all. Yes, it may feel a bit like white water rafting, but the rapids do come to an end in time.

When to Get Help

Support groups are the best for sharing this experience.

If you're concerned, talk to a grief counselor or your clergy, who can put your fears to rest by helping you see how normal your experience is.

If you have a pre-existing psychiatric disorder, stay in treatment with your mental health practitioner.

Difficulty Getting Along with Your Family

When a family member has died, losing the support of other family members feels like an additional loss.

It's your family who should be there for you, right? Actually, when it comes to grief, the answer is often no. When it comes to grief, other family members are often the last people who can support you.

They can't support you because they are grieving too. It is precisely because you've shared this loss that you can't support each other as fully as you might in another situation. Your husband, wife, children or siblings are hurting every bit as much as you are, which means they have no emotional reserves left to support you, and you don't have the emotional reserves to support them.

We get pretty darn self-absorbed when we're grieving. That's exactly how it's supposed to be, but it does create the potential for conflict and misunderstanding. It's so easy to make the assumption that everyone else is feeling what we're feeling when we're feeling it, so it's easy to assume that just because you're feeling sad, angry, guilty, anxious, or relieved, that everyone else is too...but they are not.

The hurt and tension resulting from making these kinds of assumptions can be devastating. Recognize that your family members are grieving too and their grief will not be a duplicate of yours. This is why friends and support groups are so important. You do need to look outside the family for support.

The key here is to understand and acknowledge what's going on. You still love your family, but you may not be able to share your grief with them in the ways you'd like. Give it time and let everyone follow their own path. In the meantime, look for support outside your family.

Where families can be helpful is in the shared storytelling and remembrances from your life with the person who died, but even here, not everyone may be ready to participate and share in this way at the same time.

Another aspect of not getting along with family has to do with displaced grief. It is so easy to find other things to distract us from our feelings. This can be especially true around money. Arguments about money and possessions are often more an expression of grief than of any real issues about money.

Recently, I was called for jury duty on a case where the siblings were actually in court arguing over their mother's will three years after her death. If you're headed down this road, knock it off. It's not about the money. It's about your grief.

If there are disagreements about money or possessions, wait for at least a year before making any decisions. It takes longer than that for a will to clear probate so there's really no rush. There's a good chance you'll be able to work things out once your grief doesn't feel so raw.

When to Get Help

Get support from outside your family. Often a trusted friend will be enough. Other times, support groups will fill the need.

If the family dynamics are issues of long standing, the grief may be an opening to heal them. Consulting a grief counselor is often helpful.

No matter what the situation, get a lawyer to handle the will and probate. If there's an inheritance, get sound financial advice as well.

Being Afraid You'll Forget Them

Immediately following a death, you may think of little else than the person who died.

Thoughts and feelings about your loss can be all-consuming for the first few months following a death. Often, these thoughts are a comfort because they help us feel connected to the person who died.

As time passes, you'll notice that minutes, hours and even days may go by when you don't think about the person at all. Some people find this upsetting because it feels like they're forgetting the person who died. You are not! When you stop thinking about them every minute of every day, it means you're healing.

The constant and recurring thoughts in early grief are about loss. They're about trying to come to terms with loss. Over time, no matter how profound the loss, you will come to a place of acceptance. As you become less focused on the loss, you actually become more focused on the love. With that shift, the thoughts about loss diminish and are replaced by true remembrance.

The thoughts and feelings which endure are very much like the thoughts and feelings we had while they were alive. Realizing we don't think about anyone all the time when they're alive helps many people dispel the notion that somehow we should be thinking about them all the time after they die.

If you're afraid of forgetting the person you love, I'd suggest intentionally creating a small ritual of remembrance like looking at their picture every morning, going to the cemetery once a week, or including them in your prayers.

When to Get Help

If you're hanging on to your grief as a way of staying connected to the person who died, talk to your clergy or a grief counselor.

After the first year or so, if you're still not thinking about anything other than the person who died, I would encourage you to consult a grief counselor.

Insensitive Comments from Others

This is a hot topic in most support groups.

Death makes people uncomfortable - period. Because they're so uncomfortable and don't know what to say, they say the most insensitive, hurtful and stupid things. Anyone who has grieved has heard it.

It may not be possible to isolate yourself entirely from people suffering from foot-in-mouth disease, but you can and should limit your contact. There may be friends you just can't be around right now. That's OK. It's up to you to decide who to spend time with and who not to spend time with.

Though it may seem selfish, it is not. This is a time for taking extremely good care of yourself and spending time with people who don't understand how to be supportive is not taking good care of yourself.

You don't need consolation or sympathy, and you certainly don't need pity. What you do need are friends who can stand with you without flinching. You need friends who can listen and witness your grief without trying to fix it. You need friends you will listen to the stories you have to tell.

Friends like that can be hard to find, which is why support groups are so important. I can't encourage you enough to go to a support group where you can find the kind of friends you really need right now.

When to Get Help

Limiting your social network to trusted friends and joining a support group is all that's required here.

People Worrying about You

Sometimes, well meaning friends or family will worry about how well you're doing, or not.

Many people have an extremely distorted sense of what your grief should look like and how long it should take. Remember that you are the ultimate authority about your own grief. As long as you are allowing yourself to grieve and the process is moving, you're undoubtedly doing just fine.

Often someone else's concern about you is a way of avoiding their own grief. It's easier to worry about you than deal with their own feelings. Worry is a way of trying to control a situation, so worry about you may be an attempt on their part (albeit unconsciously) to control and contain their own grief.

If you're a family member reading this, this is the criteria to use. Is Mom all over the map? Is Dad's grief changing over time? If it feels fluid, there's nothing to worry about even if it does seem prolonged to you. In the meantime, attend to your own grieving process which may be taking a very different path.

When to Get Help

No interventions necessary here. Joining a support group is often helpful because they all understand what you're going through.

If you suspect other people may be right, consult a grief counselor.

Pressure to Move On

People around you may pressure you to move on. The funeral's over, it's time to get on with your life, right? Wrong! Again, this is rooted in their own discomfort. Your grief is just too close. After all, it could be them who lost someone they love.

The only person who can tell you when it's time to move on is you. Chances are, you will begin to move on before you even realize that you have. That's how it generally works.

Sometimes the pressure comes from within. Shouldn't you be over this already? No. Grief cannot be rushed. Grief takes time, and our job is to follow where it leads.

It won't always be the wailing pain kind of grief. You'll go through many variations on a theme. Regardless of the path your grief takes, you will eventually come to a place of peace with a renewed capacity to move into a new and fulfilling life.

This takes time and will not happen in the first few days, weeks or months of your grief. How long varies so much from person to person that putting a time frame on it isn't helpful. The real key to whether your grief is on track is if it feels like a dynamic, fluid experience.

When to Get Help

If you have any doubts about whether what you're

experiencing is normal, talk with your clergy, a grief counselor or join a support group. Anyone who understands grieving can help you understand whether your grief is normal or whether you are getting stuck.

Living in the Past

During the first few months following a loss, it's common to focus on the life that was rather than the life that is. It is normal to be focused on all of the events that led up to the death. It's normal to be thinking and talking about them for many months following a death.

This is usually a way of processing what's happened since it takes a while for our minds to catch up to the reality of the present. Other times, we may cling to the past as a way of staying connected to the person who died. (See *Being Afraid You'll Forget Them*).

For others, it may be a way of avoiding the grief. It can be easier to focus on the past than to feel the pain of the present. That makes a lot of sense when you think about it. The hardest period of time in the grieving process happens in the middle where the death has become real, but we're not ready to start thinking about the future. That period of time can feel particularly bleak. Unfortunately, avoiding it generally prolongs the agony.

You are probably the only person who can say for sure whether living in the past is just a part of the process or an attempt to avoid the pain of the present. Do be honest with yourself and remember the fastest way through your grief is to feel it and follow it. Trying to force yourself forward prematurely is as difficult as trying to slow the process down. The key is to allow your grief to unfold as it needs.

When to Get Help

If you feel you're getting stuck in the past, talk to your clergy or a grief counselor. It can be really difficult to evaluate our own progress while we're in the middle of, so if you're not sure, ask someone who understands grief to help.

You Can't Remember Anything Bad about the Person...or Anything Good

Have you ever noticed how someone dies and suddenly they become larger than life? Somehow their less than beautiful traits disappear the moment they die, and we begin to remember them in an idealized fashion.

Sometimes, this is coming from cultural messages about not speaking ill of the dead, but more often, we really only remember the good things. Having this kind of selective amnesia is normal, especially in the first few months following the death.

Over time, this idealized version is replaced by memories of the real person in all of their humanness...the beautiful, the un-beautiful, the quirks that really weren't so endearing, and those that were. This is when you know you're beginning to heal, because healing from a loss like this means remembering them as they really were...all of it.

Sometimes, if the relationship was particularly traumatic, the reverse can be true. All you can remember are all the awful things that were said or done.

In this case, you are grieving more than just the death. You are also grieving the relationship which was never what you wanted it to be, and you're grieving the loss of hope that it might get better.

Whichever way your memory goes, the road to recovery and

resolution remains the same...to embrace the person fully in their humanity...the good, the bad, and the ugly.

When to Get Help

If you had a difficult relationship with the person who died, talk with a grief counselor. Situations in which this might be the case include relationships that involve abandonment; emotional, physical or sexual abuse; or drug and alcohol addiction. If those situations apply, your grief is much more complicated and multifaceted, and I would recommend getting help in dealing with it.

Feeling Overwhelmed

Feeling overwhelmed is most common immediately following a death but can continue throughout the grieving process.

Part of the overwhelm is that you may be facing many new experiences. Spouses who relied on a partner may find cooking, home repairs, or finances a daily exercise in frustration and overwhelm.

Legal and financial challenges are often a source of overwhelm. Just finding the will can be challenging for some, never mind dealing with changes to bank accounts, probate and all the rest.

Then there's the emotional overwhelm. Grief takes all of our energy so even the most routine tasks seem like a burden. Simple things like taking a shower or cooking a meal can just feel like too much trouble.

This is all so normal and resolves over time. You will learn the new skills you need to know, the financial issues will resolve, and the emotional overwhelm will diminish over time.

As your grief resolves and you master new skills, it's common to feel exhilarated by having successfully met all the challenges the loss of a family member or spouse presents. Yes, it may feel like a bit of a consolation prize because you'd give it all up in a minute if you could have them back. What you get instead is the experience of being a resourceful and resilient human being, and that's worth knowing.

When to Get Help

Ask for help when you need it. Your friends often don't know how to help once the funeral's over. Help them help you by asking. Whether it's learning to cook, learning how to balance your checkbook, or dealing with the car mechanic, there are undoubtedly people around you who would love to help you. Let them.

For legal and financial issues, get a lawyer and accountant. Not only are these issues usually beyond our experience and expertise, but even if you have the knowledge, chances are, you are not clear-headed enough to deal with estate issues alone.

Money / Changes in Spending Habits

This one is multilayered. Some of it is legal and some of it is emotional.

Death can trigger a financial crisis, sometimes real and sometimes not. Whether a crisis or not, money does come into play when somebody dies. This can trigger lots of fear and uncertainty. If there's money coming to you, it may feel overwhelming.

Changes in spending habits can be a way of coping with the intensity of your feelings. Going on a spending spree can feel invigorating and enlivening, a reaffirmation of life.

Or, you may find yourself penny pinching in response to a death, especially if you were financially dependent on the person who died.

Generally, changes in spending habits are short lived. A single shopping spree is of little consequence. A bit of penny pinching until you regain your emotional or financial equilibrium isn't generally harmful.

Unless you're really putting yourself at continued financial risk or physical harm (like not eating to save money), I wouldn't worry much about this one.

When to Get Help

Get a good attorney to take care of the legal issues. Let your attorney guide you to the right kind of financial advice for your personal situation and use it. This is one area where going it alone is not a good idea.

Generally, changes in spending habits are short lived with no harm done. If you're putting yourself at financial risk or engaged in other kinds of destructive behavior, get thee to a grief counselor ASAP.

Sadness and Depression

Forgive me for stating the obvious, but sadness is a normal part of grief.

At times, especially in the first few months, the sadness feels unrelenting and overwhelming, but even in the midst of the bone deep sadness of grief, there will be moments of bittersweet relief when you remember something funny about the person who died.

Periods of depression are a normal part of grief, but what distinguishes them from a clinical depression is that they really are just periods of depression, not an ongoing state that lasts for months.

Although grief can cause symptoms similar to depression as evidenced by this list, that doesn't mean it is. It's important to recognize the difference between a genuine clinical depression and grief.

Depression is a chemical imbalance in the brain...it is a disorder that needs treatment. There's a good chance, you have had episodes of depression prior to this death, and it is certainly possible for a loss of this kind to trigger a depressive episode. If you have a history of depression, stay in treatment.

On the other hand, grief is not a disorder. It is a normal response to a traumatic loss, and does not require clinical treatment. Grief will do the healing in its' own way, in its' own time. There is an inherent wisdom about grief that heals our hearts in much the same way our bodies heal from physical injury. The most important thing you can do is to let the process unfold as it needs.

The chief indicator here is not a diagnostic manual, but rather how fluid your grief is. Normal grief is all over the map. It comes in waves. You're up and down. Your feelings can be quite strong and contradictory. And over time, it changes, often very subtly at first, but it changes.

Though depression can certainly be cyclical it doesn't generally cycle through as quickly as grief, which tends to be much more moment to moment. With depression, there tends to be a more muted quality as opposed to the explosive and brilliant emotions of grief. Depression takes root in a way that grief does not. Even though you may feel like it's never going to end when you're grieving, it does.

When to Get Help

Get help if your depression persists over time without any change or let up. Also get help if you're exhibiting classic signs of depression for more than a few days at a time...not getting out of bed, not getting dressed, not tending to personal hygiene, not eating, etc.

If you're still worried about it, check it out. Put your mind at ease instead of worrying and wondering by consulting a mental health professional who specializes in grief.

Get help if you're thinking about suicide. That's depression, and it is important to let somebody know.

If you are in an emergency situation, CALL 911 or go to your nearest emergency room.

A Crisis in Faith / Changes in Your Religious or Spiritual Practice

It is very common for the death of someone you love to trigger a crisis in faith.

For some, a death becomes a spiritual crisis, causing you to turn away from past beliefs and practices. For others, a death can be an opening to spiritual and religious curiosity. And for others, a loss challenges your beliefs in a way that reaffirms and deepens your spiritual or religious experience.

Some typical scenarios are...

• Being a regular participant who finds yourself questioning God, even being angry at God, for letting the person you love die. Some stop attending church, temple, or mosque altogether, while others stop for a time.

• Lapsed practitioners experience renewed interest and participation in their previous spiritual or religious practice.

• A death may trigger a spiritual awakening for some who have never really considered such matters before this loss.

Despite the many preconceived ideas we carry with us, all spiritual growth involves periods of serious doubt, and sometimes, outright rejection of previously held beliefs. Doesn't it make sense that the death of someone you love might propel you into deep questioning about life, death, and God?

I can't answer the questions for you, but I will say that God can take whatever we have to dish out. One of the most memorable experiences from my support group days was listening to the Catholic priest whose sister had dropped dead of a heart attack at age 35. He was very, very angry at God. What was such a gift to all of us, was how freely he shared his anger and his doubts, giving everyone permission to do the same. In time, the anger and doubts resolved, and he emerged with a much deeper understanding of his faith, which in turn, enhanced his ability to minister to others.

Just as allowing your grief to be exactly what it is diminishes the pain and speeds the process, so does being comfortable with the discomfort of having your belief system challenged. It can be tremendously painful and can be experienced as yet another loss, but these 'dark night of the soul' experiences call on us to sit with the confusion, to be with the questions without trying to nail down the answers prematurely.

Most people find reading, writing and meditation or prayer to be the most helpful during this time.

When to Get Help

Talk with your clergy if you find this helpful. Good ones will always make room for your doubts.

Guilt

A variety of issues can come up following a death to elicit guilt. Two of the most common are not having done enough in caring for the person who died or having unfinished business with them.

After a lengthy illness, those left behind often experience guilt about not having done enough to take care of the person who has died. Sometimes, this can be as extreme as feeling guilt about not having been able to save them.

It's really important to realize there was very little you could have done differently. You certainly weren't responsible for their illness, and you did the very best you could in an impossible situation. Taking care of someone who's dying is physically and emotionally draining. There is no way anyone is going to do it perfectly.

A variation on this is feeling guilty for not getting them to the doctor sooner or guilt about not getting them to take better care of themselves. Though understandable, you need to remember that you were not the one responsible for those decisions.

When your relationship with the person who died was difficult, there is often unfinished business. Although not the only response to unfinished business, guilt is a common one. Guilt that you didn't make peace with them, guilt that you didn't say all you wanted to say, and guilt for any harm you think you may have caused.

Often, you may experience guilt and anger simultaneously; anger at them for their part in the difficulty, and guilt for your part.

Depending on the severity of the difficulty and the intensity of your response, this kind of guilt may go beyond normal grief. Anytime you're grieving a death and the loss of a hoped for relationship, your grief becomes more complicated.

It's certainly normal to look back with a critical eye on what you said and did. When not confronting death, we tend to believe we have an unlimited number of redos. After someone has died, we realize there's no going back. This realization alone can bring on a feeling of guilt.

Regardless of the cause, guilt needs to be acknowledged.

Forgiveness is the answer but it can't be forced. Give it time. Be open to forgiveness but don't try to forgive yourself or the other person before you're really ready. To force it tends to create a spiral into more guilt because you think you should be able to forgive, but you can't.

When to Get Help

Talk to a grief counselor if you have unfinished business, your relationship was particularly difficult, or you're consumed with guilt. Getting this kind of help will allow you to heal more completely and more quickly than if you try go it alone.

Having Trouble Remembering
What They Looked Like or Sounded Like

Many people find this phenomenon quite disturbing when it's really just a function of how memory works. Despite deep love and long association, the mental memory of what any person looks like or sounds tends to get foggy over time. This is true of people who are still alive.

As much as not being able to conjure up these physical memories feels like more loss and some sort of failure on your part, it is not. You really do remember them. You would recognize them immediately if they came back to life, and you do recognize them every time you look at photographs, videos, or listen to recordings. That's remembering them, but it's not the memory that really counts.

Although most of us can't remember exactly what they looked like when we think about them, we do remember the relationship, which is what we've really lost. The memory that really counts is the memory we hold in our hearts. That memory is about the love we shared and is one we never forget, not ever.

A death after a lengthy illness presents a particular challenge when it comes to memories of the person who died. Immediately following the death, recalling memories from before the illness can be quite difficult. You want to remember them as they were when they were well, but all you seem to remember is how they looked at the end. The fear, of course, is that this is what you're going to be left with. It is not.

The grieving process is about weaving together all of the memories and experiences you had with the person who died. Although you'll never forget the illness or the situation surrounding their death, that is only a small part of your entire relationship. More recent memories always claim our attention for a time but then they blend into the tapestry that makes up an entire relationship.

Sharing stories, home movies and photo albums are all ways of remembering the relationship that lives on in your heart as well as the physical reality of what they looked and sounded like.

When to Get Help

Support groups are the best for this kind of thing.

Conclusion

Even if you have every response listed above, it doesn't mean anything other than you're grieving.

Conflicting responses are very common. Common examples are anger and guilt, relief and sadness, tears and laughter, or even being glad they're no longer suffering and feeling sorry for yourself. We are complex beings, capable of holding great paradox, especially when it comes to our experiences of loss. The work of grief is to weave it all together into a coherent whole.

I've said it before, but I will say it again; the most accurate criteria to access whether what you're experiencing is normal, is how fluid it feels. Despite the attempts to describe grief in stages and tasks, there are no arbitrary markers more effective than this sense of movement. As long as your grief is moving and your responses change over time, you can be assured what you're experiencing is normal.

THINGS YOU CAN DO
TO PROMOTE HEALING

The most important thing you can do is to allow yourself to feel it all. There will be times you will just shut down because it's too much to bear. That's okay, but the more you can come back to it and stay with it, the faster and more completely you will heal.

Here are some tried and true methods to help you navigate your grieving process.

• *Take good care of yourself*
It's hard and you won't always succeed, but try to take really good care of yourself by getting enough sleep, eating well, exercising. All the things we're supposed to be doing anyway, become especially important now.

• *Trust the process*
I know that's easier said than done, but grief really does know the way and will prove to be your most trustworthy companion. Your grief will lead you exactly where you need to go and will protect you when you just can't take anymore. Having experienced it myself, and having sat with many people through this process, I'm here to tell you there is no way you can improve on the process.

• *Cultivate an open heart*
Rather than shutting down around your emotions, embrace them. Acceptance that this is where you are and what you're

feeling will go a long way toward moving the process along. Even in the midst of chaos and conflict, the heart has the capacity to sit with the great paradox of life and death.

• Be selfish

I mean that in the best possible sense of the word. This is a time for you to be doing what you need for yourself, not for other people. You are the ultimate authority on your own process and you know better than anyone else exactly what you need. Rather than following the advice of others, listen to your own internal voice.

• Create rituals

These don't have to be the formal rituals of religious practice, though they can be. Rituals can be as simple as sitting with a picture of your loved one every morning and talking to them. You are only limited by your imagination, but some rituals others have found helpful include embracing the clothes that still carry the person's scent, visiting the cemetery, going to church, writing letters to the person, lighting candles, and setting aside an hour a day to feel miserable before getting on with your day.

• Write

There's a reason there are so many published memoirs about grief. Writing works.

You don't need to write a memoir, but journal writing can be immensely healing. One of the things we need most is to tell our stories about the person who died, our relationship with them, and our experience of losing them. Friends can get mighty tired of listening to the same story over and over. Journals never do. When the story starts boring you, you'll know you're moving forward.

Letter writing, too, can be healing, especially when there were things left unsaid or when you had a difficult relationship with the person who died. Writing to them, saying what you need to say, telling them how you really feel, can all be accomplished through writing letters. Even better than talking to them which can also work, letters concretize it all in a way that makes letting go easier.

• *Talk*

Whether talking to friends, a support group, a counselor, or your clergy, talking, getting it all out no matter how silly or stupid it may seem, is healing. The process of saying it and having someone actively listen without trying to fix it can make all the difference.

For many people, talking to the person who died is also helpful.

• *Share memories*

When possible, remembering stories with other family members and friends can be incredibly healing. When people come together to remember, it's like the person comes alive for us. In sharing the memories, we begin to realize they live on in the hearts and minds of everyone who loved them.

Stories of this kind have been shared since the birth of

human beings. In recent years, online memorials have become another way of sharing. They may not replace direct human contact, but having a forum to tell your story can be immensely healing.

• Exercise

Even under the best of circumstances, many of us resist this, but physical exertion can do much to dispel painful emotions. This is especially true when we feel like we're stuck, spinning around in the same emotional stew. Going for a brisk walk can get things moving again.

• Meditation and Prayer

Whether you consider yourself religious or not, meditation and prayer decreases stress and helps us open up to what we're feeling.

• Do Something Fun

No matter how all encompassing this experience may be, there are times when you just need a break. Renting a funny movie can be just the thing to distract you for a bit. Playing with kids or animals can have a similar effect. Whatever activities you find fun, make sure you do them from time to time.

• Spend time with friends

Not all friends are good company right now. Those who are uncomfortable, judgmental, or only want to talk about their experience are best avoided. Spend time with friends who get it and are willing to understand. These are the friends who are ready and willing to listen, and are also willing to do something else besides talking about your grief.

• Keep their things around

Especially keep their picture around where you can see it often. Some people think it's better to clear out everything that reminds them of the person. Even if you have the impulse to clear out, don't do it immediately. Having clothes, personal items, and photographs around can be very comforting. There is no rush. You'll know when it's time to clear out the clothes, but the photographs will undoubtedly stay out for many years to come.

• Join a support group

Almost every community has one. Check with your local hospice program or funeral home for a referral.

Many people resist this, but I have to say it is one of the most profoundly healing things you can do for yourself. For most people, sitting with others who've experienced a similar loss, can be a huge relief.

A support group gives you the opportunity to be with others who really understand what it is you're going through. You get to see how other people are moving through the process which normalizes your own. As new people join the group, you gain a point of reference to see how far you've really come.

Support groups can be a real life line when family and friends can't be there for you.

The best time to join is 3- 6 months after the death, or when the shock starts wearing off. Personally, I think bereavement support groups are the most effective support anyone can have.

• Look for the Gifts

I don't mean to suggest you should be a Pollyanna about it, but I've never talked to anyone who hasn't felt there were great gifts for them in this process. Everyone says the price wasn't worth it, but if they had to lose the person they loved, they are glad for the lessons they've learned and the gifts their grief has given them. Stay open to the gifts.

• Avoid making any major life decisions during the first year following a death

There is no rush. You're too disoriented to be making those kinds of decisions right now. Take your time and don't allow anyone else to rush you.

WHEN TO GET HELP

Although most of what is experienced during the grieving process is quite normal, there are situations that make grief more complicated. Complicated grief is virtually impossible to heal without some outside help.

The following situations are the kind that complicate grief. If they apply to you, I strong encourage you to talk with a grief counselor or your clergy.

• If **the death was particularly traumatic** such as homicide, suicide, or accident.

• If you've had **multiple losses in close succession.**

• If the current loss is bringing up **unresolved issues from a previous loss.**

• If **you feel suicidal.** This is especially true if you find yourself thinking about how you might do it.

It's normal to wonder how you'll ever go on, but it is not normal to think about joining your loved one. You may have flashes of wishing you were the one who had died. Or you might have a stray thought about how it would be easier if you were dead. That's all normal. **What's not normal is to be thinking about it a lot, and making plans to do it. If you cross the line, please get some help.**

National Suicide Prevention Lifeline
http://www.suicidepreventionlifeline.org/
1-800-273-8255

Suicide Prevention Center
http://www.suicidepreventioncenter.org/
1-877-784-2433

If you are in an emergency situation, call 911 or go to your nearest emergency room.

• If you're engaging in self destructive behavior like driving fast or carelessly, drinking to excess, drugging (including unprescribed or excessive use of prescription drugs), overspending, or engaging in other risky behavior, particularly when you can't seem to stop.

• When there were other problems in the relationship, such as it was a bad marriage, a child estranged from a parent, or abuse was a factor. The more difficult the relationship, the harder the grief because you're grieving the actually loss of the person and the hoped for relationship that is now irrevocably lost to you. If you were in an abusive relationship with the person who died, you may experience rage that you can no longer confront them. This is not normal grief.

• If you can't stop crying. Tears are normal but they come and go. It's normal for tears to be triggered many times during the day, but normally, the tears come and then they pass until the next time. If you can't stop crying at all, get some help.

• **If you aren't sleeping at all.** Having trouble sleeping is normal and not a reason for concern. Typically, you'll have trouble falling asleep but will drift off for a few hours at least. Or you may fall asleep, but after a few hours, you're wide awake. That's normal, but if you find you really aren't sleeping at all, every night, all night long for days on end, it's probably time to get some help.

• If you feel like you are reliving the same thing over and over for days, weeks or months without the slightest change, the same feelings, dreams, images, behaviors. **Normal grief is fluid and changing. If it doesn't feel fluid, it's time to get some help.**

• Any time **you're seriously questioning your responses.** Although grief may be a new experience for you, you are still the best authority on you. If you suspect something isn't normal, check it out. Better to know so your worry doesn't get mixed in with the grief.

WHERE TO GET HELP

• Your **local hospice** is probably your best resource. Even if the death you experienced was sudden, your local hospice will have a complete list of local support groups and grief counselors.

• **Funeral homes** are well versed on grief and often provide educational support to the community. They are also likely to have a list of support groups and counselors who are available for your support.

• Local **mental health clinics** also provide services. Just make sure that whoever you consult is really an expert in grief.

• Your local **clergy** is usually a good resource. Even if you aren't a member, most clergy are happy to help anyone in need.

• Your **physician** may be able to refer you to the appropriate group or counselor. The problem with many physicians is they are way too willing to prescribe medication without adequate assessment.

SUGGESTED READING

This is a short list of books consistently reported as being helpful:

Grollman, Earl, Living When a Loved One has Died, Boston: Beacon Press, 1977.

Krementz, Jill, How it Feels When A Parent Dies, New York: Knopf, 1981.

Kushner, Harold: When Bad Things Happen To Good People, Avon, 1983.

Levine, Stephen, Who Dies? An Investigation of Conscious Living and Conscious Dying, Garden City, NY: Anchor Press/Doubleday, 1982.

Lewis, C.S. A Grief Observed, New York: The Seabury Press, 1961.

Noel, Brook & Blair, Pamela D. I Wasn't Ready to Say Goodbye: surviving, coping & healing after the sudden death of a loved one, Milwaukee, Champion Press, 2000.

Rando, T. How to Go on Living When Someone You Love Dies, Lexington, MA: Lexington Books, 1988

Tatelbaum, Judy, The Courage to Grieve, New York: Lippincott and Crowell, 1980.

Temes, Roberta, _Living with an Empty Chair_, New York: Irvington Publishers, 1977.

ONLINE RESOURCES

A wonderful interactive program can be found at:
Myselfhelp.com
http://www.myselfhelp.com/Programs/CWG.html

Two good articles on grief, can be found at:
Hospice - A Guide To Grief
http://hospicenet.org/html/grief_guide.html
Hospice - Knowledge
http://hospicenet.org/html/knowledge.html

A list of grief resources provided by the National Funeral Directors Association:
Grief-Relation Information and Organizations
http://www.nfda.org/relatedsites.php#Grief

More resources including links for help following a murder or suicide provided by University of Virginia Health Services:
National Bereavement Resources
http://www.healthsystem.virginia.edu/internet/chaplaincy/bereavement/national.cfm

For support following the loss of a child:
The Compassionate Friends
http://www.compassionatefriends.org/

For support following a traumatic death:
The Center for Traumatic Grief and Victim Services
http://www.traumaticgrief.org/

Susan's Story

I went back to school following my mother's death in 1985. I wanted to work for hospice because hospice and a local support group had been my lifelines during her illness. I felt a deep calling to the work. My academic advisers wouldn't let me do it for 2 years, but in the end, I did my internship at a local hospice.

Upon completion of my Master's Degree in counseling psychology, I facilitated a bereavement support group at Omega Emotional Support Services. I credit the 3 years I spent with this group for making me an expert on grief. We met every other week and would have anywhere from 10-25 people dropping in to share their vast and varied experiences.

My understanding was deepened by my work with hospice, where I trained volunteers in grief support and provided bereavement services to hospice families. The passage from life into death is a sacred moment. I left hospice in 1994 because it was just becoming too normal, and I was losing my sense of the sacred.

Soon after leaving hospice, I was called upon to be the primary caregiver for my father who died of Alzheimer's disease in 2003.

Though less of a daily event, I didn't give up the work with grief entirely. As a psychotherapist specializing in grief counseling, I continued my support for people who were grieving, and did so for over 17 years. Although I no longer practice, I still hold a license as a Licensed Mental Health Counselor (LMHC) in the Commonwealth of Massachusetts.

I now live in Rhode Island with my golden retriever, Heidi, where just for a change of pace, I provide personal, business and creative coaching to artists, artisans, and writers.

To join a 'Survive Your Grief Support Group', please contact me at

susan@susanfuller.com

To order addtional copies. please visit me at:

http://www.SurviveYourGrief.com

Made in the USA
Lexington, KY
17 February 2011